SEVLESMEHT

AND THE BIRDS

~previewing the special body (DNE)~

t thilleman

Spuyten Duyvil   New York City

Library of Congress Cataloging-in-Publication Data

Thilleman, Tod.
  Sevlesmeht and the birds : previewing the special
body (dne) / T. Thilleman.
     pages ; cm. -- (Anatomical sketches ; Book 6)
  ISBN 978-1-941550-19-9
  1. Experimental fiction. I. Title.
  PS3570.H453S49 2015
  813'.54--dc23
                                    2014034398

Deluded natures cannot recognize
The royal way that stands before their eyes.
Farīd ud-Dīn ʿAṭṭār, *The Conference of the Birds*

DUCTUS UPDRAFT

Great dark parsimony   catenating
                    compounded wings a watery squeal-
Ing expenditure   releases up-drafting fat fanning
Blades flapping the billowing residue   flocks
                          smoke smotes the desert sky
Blotted landscape
Murmurrating hybrids
            specie uncashed
Pre-existent spreads beginning sight blinds
Always the eye's flight
Values
              without sight
History the ocular activity plotted in memorial registers

Focuses interior image
            squalling conference accumulates thru image
Resource hears abundant captivated wealth   interconnected
Serenely raging waves sways tonal vibration
                        algorithms from available aetherial dusk

Fire
       off this Earth
                         heat mirage atmosphere fuels
Carbon
         cacophonous beaks
Crowd-sourcing changes
Rise
           massing immanent
Clear dimension an apparent upper heaven illusional

           spatial montage lands in air one moment
               losing assumed ground philogenetically owned lifetimes

Congregations   blots   conferencing
Concentrated delivery of signal
Under oceanic emissarial emissions bellow
High-pitched semblance sight captured first

Commences creatures unknowingly
    eternal fund
       communal activation
           sputtering flame's one flare
             universe's
                conceived knowing acknowledgment

Gestational   correspondent chemical   dirt or ash recognizes

Whorling up constellate's curious flue

Bones
        sweat
blood
        skin

Coagulates
        essence indissoluble future writes burningly
                glimpse incorporates
Prophetic sources gaze upon
                fueled by god-like matters
Spheric appointments
Sun in every world possible exploded
Plains give away from distance
            planes and objectives
                giving away secret codes
Orbed molecular recapitulation dissolves retrospectively

Ur-sight sound and long
Unwinding thread
    light's movement wound profundity

        night's

first sketch]

        SEVLESMEHT enters shaman's tent-cave to light the fire
finding flame never gone out   of course   fuels   the very matter of all
dead things one day visits this special flame only in history we've written so far
heat   more essence lights   unseen torch bears each scene   up the
middle   newest exile   gesture's furthest realization

THERSEYN he envisions   out of all has caused him or did not cause to be here

     he   must attach to other fuel   scraps otherwise keep him an
outrider   his attempt at interpretation lost   gathered into meditation

     rumor of his own body ritual about to come upon
presence never before quite this shadow

     focused by exile
     knowing body's resource   hand now up
     skull
     out of migration eclipsing scattering

     RED CIVILIZATIONS   threads

     nothing but several Gods of drama   war

     crackling burning

Seen / Un Seen

The end came to civilized embodiments
      receptors enshrined enslaved   pawn or God

At last   total flailing incapacity insubordinate

                  Earth
                    insubordinate celestial fire
                        underneath PLNIPLOI's coup

      true image   finally human
                       withdrew
    to invert summation   twilight feature
                bodily render eternity
    churning depths for infinite unknown transmission

PLNIPLOI   navel out of which the angel of human resource
          passes into rendition of all false historicals
               at one with the un-warring specter of himself
         trumps without struggle image without matter
           figuration of limited vocabularies unable to access
               fuel   cold and isolated as death's own

weather   cemetery cemented
dis-ease ever rises to overcome

These   written circulations   recalled THERSEYN
so that minor characters continue
the human door

PLINIPLOI
gathered into grip
defining eternity as that can only be taught

Passing inheritance what uninstructed
he becomes
symbolic captivity
knowledge
uses up

AVISTAVARZERVAIRYU   born from this still point
oracular glistening drop of falling celestial tones

SHIRU heard

brings limited time historical fictions

S H E wed to hypostatical end of PLNIPLOI
cannot understand
uprisen insurrects self to be her challenge
ignorant to the infinite garment
spun from star RORZHNAN
carries inception of all age's believable

THERSEYN
related her appearance
so that minor to major
which music PLNIPLOI's age might emerge meaningful

AVISTAVARZERVAIRYU
manifests ages   stages
circularity holds
upon sky SEVLESMEHT be-holds
His wonder heretofore unattributable
role-playing vanished and assumed
sight sees him
beginning synonymous
to fire we hear
out of endless
burning limit

second sketch]

                   of our understanding the crossing ribbon of space the circular
nature of what we once named time   engaging movements moments land itself
re-formed   before   it entered eternality the light of fire was   mixing
smoke light brought the aspect of PLNIPLOI   a capture of revelation light
has in fire   captured smoke circling doubt   abyss not apprehended
light not to be released

                                      true as long as
SEVLESMEHT can remember but he has no memory anymore   no people
no job or practice   empire of ZAS and MOIRA undone by their child
PLNIPLOI as well as other disintegrations over-use under-utilization
         a premise   subduing actual Earth   as other   planets
will be   sub-servient creatures life-forms clinging to each
and every planet subdued   basest most elemental appearance has not yet
been seen   the greater struggle
                         Self comes under presumption   but
also to valuations of continual burning flame contains light
                      the entire body humans
        direct transmission
                  toward the eye
                          captures   written
memorized turned over and over formed heavens up above the up above believe it
or not this errant philosopher SEVLESMEHT   changed by way   shaman
changing roles   Sophia's echoic parameter
          he   all at once   smoke fire light
transmission dependent on transposition of the mythic one   fact of the Other

his position nature   easily
thought belonging to person also angelic discovery in depths of what alchemical
foundations the Zoroastrian Magi of the Hellenes   meaning
        confluence of Pythagorean nature-lovers out of
storied time came to be known   Zoroaster   *Zaratos* the mis-interpreter
the Greek name the prophet or deity the access point to godhead time fire and
light   once again Pythagoreans' incessant probing of nature cosmos
perpetrate from east to west the figure of the Chaldean (Babylonian) Magus and
introduce mythic origins into the Greek world-view
        all told it

is sourced to the Avesta language textually introducing *Zervan*   shows
growth migration a bifurcated meaning the high priest a sort of fallen prophet
laws strictly esoteric   hence Orpheus holds Zervan his source
in the embodiment of verse song sung re-projection elemental originary
manifestation

        cosmicity penetrates legal identifications
we here consider as our own origins   translated by Orphic mouth
   στόμα
       individual truly emits existence given to meditation upon this
one-time allegory of time
     by which to understand leap as THERSEYN had   into
sublime all-encompassing void   holds destiny   holds   light
     (but these were teachings watered down into absence of
religion itself the uprising of the age of ZAS MOIRA the rumors of AHNÁHR and
SHIRU the intimations of EKSTONISTIAN and THERSEYN

                              then
    dynamic prophecy   he   living ribbon of codes   infra-entangled
essence inferred *enfer-red*

                  gateway land as struggle to overcome "self"   en-used by
psychic nearness   long hidden possessions

                        seeming   seaming   seams each self   re-
cording their crossing   roads   flames and tongues

XZIDYAZAG

poured out mother fire
beauty known only in image
forested hidden regions
Came to embody form's own transcendence
not so much in personation of form
but infinite reach this world only knew

twinned

Pregnancies   light and dark
manifesting angels   times and ages
incestual   progenerative
seen unknown visitations of light
erecting dark paths in this only world

And this   angel   she
above others the new
intelligence of angels
chivalrous inside subsequent sufferings
schools of overlapped labials burst from form

inevitably succumb to laughter   ridicule
the end   the lie the trick
torn from high notions

beauty seen then
absolute abstract
ugly rejected by present states of knowing

Casts an entire species ensures orders   hierarchies
         ladders   views   imprisoned prismed realities

            out the body
              his beauty

                 angles upward in drafts crossing trails

       SEVLESMEHT
    begins in waves of flame
      pictures of XZIDYAZAG's appealing
         drawing strings threads
     thru emptied mirror
             calling containment
      out of lines   frames
        curves
But sound   answering rules
        she hears he speaks
          spunk
        spoke driven words   flames
            gestate again
         enlightening

third sketch]

by leap THERSEYN pre-figured our human realm   con-
sidering age the time of SEVLESMEHT's exile   *Ahriman* arrived   in-
side the projection   Ahriman   here as SEVLESMEHT / THERSEYN duality
or twin spirit reprise out of the Gathas   anti-thesis to the leap   S. must
go the route toward discovering his seeking that leap thru peregrinating chias-
matic tongue of flame

XZIDYAZAG's arrival out of fire always has been
in the shamanic   the "modern" posture S. has as his nature
divines fire for light but can
only come to limited retarded cinema of her he has as one stage of desire
meanwhile the garment the celestial goes unheeded
believed to be where it always was in an age still contains
that gallop of historical goals and visions   (n.b.: write a prequel to the sketches
elucidating unearthed Hsian garment)

S. to come to disappointment of her as his
own creation   tho beautiful she is nowhere near perfection of aeonic
AVISTAVARZERVAIRYU

AVISTAVARZERVAIRYU
waiting specter of Ohrmazd
Ahura Mazda   the twin of celestial eternal time   dioscuri the Hellenes
fashioned withheld and potioned potented Orphic texts funeral rites   but to
no avail   history marched toward inevitable xristianization of the West (or
whatever else you want to name it)

and that is all history will ever be good for (mouth full of words) as far as these
terms are concerned   sealed away for good   surviving pre-historical
gaze now

                    looking at twins of light and dark
          out of infinite time Zervan first figure destiny precursor to
Angelic holding things in light and dark

                more to our own point the making fashioning
technics the garment celestial stole she wears

                   prophecy mantle round the
method of modernism   and in all contemporary goals the putting
together the unraveling as well   this method the method of "prophet"

sketch continued from the previous]

                             S. doesn't know this circular prophecy
so he's the exo-coital onanism of retarded or pretend vision   jumping and
moving around the fire its heat ascendance its light the kept coveted image of the
beauty of beauties

                        image now thru cycles of his own history once again
jerking him off in cinematic specter of XZIDYAZAG   til he begins to yearn
for real skin reality body partner goddess left to be only rumor image still retains

sees   yearning interpreted as PLNIPLOI   imageless   unadorned

       yearning *becomes* method urges S. once again
                 leap into immolation of the void   realize
intensity the star AVISTAVARZERVAIRYU

             takes her position of thwart   blocking
Ahriman and darkness   blots out smoke interpretive cinematics of
Ahriman   into the true age   enwrapped woven satiety the Goddess's
celestial parameter

       enveloping his whole being in stillness
            forever before
       explosion of all methodologies   girdles invention

CREATION
OF RORSHNAN's ANTECEDENT

"… it steps back to watch the forms of transcendence fly up like sparks from a fire; it slackens the intentional threads which attach us to the world and thus brings them to our notice; it alone is consciousness of the world because it reveals that world as strange and paradoxical."
Merleau-Ponty, *Phenomenology of Perception* (1945)

Living the remotest part of theater
Image flickers lighted flame
                    technique of divination
Vocabulary
            sighting constant absorption

Out of flame light one leap crossing
    fondling self-enclosure of empire
Pneuma and *Physis*

emergence an asterism unrivaled

RORZHNAN   with   AVISTAVARZERVAIRYU
SEVLESMEHT   robed
        heat-lick salving his dead conscience
                    death of his own death
        Empirical records for one
                recently ends
                        personifies disuse his

16

                    disablement
              by multitudes and masses

Up against smoke-hole projection an entire civilization
Birds   amassing
        sky hole
              part and entirety
                    sacrificed eternal rays
                          shoots weft
                    threading woof-roof

Visions martial array which ended time
Here embodiment subtle shuttle's
                    future's regained
                          origination organizing
                    ecstatic faults feeling
                                reinstituted
                    his immolation
              withinwards

Her here meaning
        removal script
                spatio-temporal infinity fittedly strange

Partnering all wearable interpretation

fourth sketch]

out of eternal-infinite place   veiled name   creation never ended

THWIILASAQBW̃

the passive tense might be companion to the active
however you want structure in the grammar of time
or literary allegorical   or performative stance surreal a(e)lludes
dimension beyond what is "known" symbolically
all have instant partnership of passive active
eyes ears see hear what each Earth gives out of aeonic voice
projectiles missiles of attention intention their procreative fully funded surge
passivity forever pressured connection to leap
origin's light first found as fund

Iblis Re-deemed: Garment of Fire

THWIILASAQBẄ throws Iblis into world

SEVLESMEHT medium of message
                 recognizing blockage   doubt
                     cinematic self-doubt
         overcomes by self-immolation over and over

Entirety of THWIILASAQBẄ
Shows Iblis

            cloud recurrence
                   past plays present
      gaming   defunding limited time
           self needs prove
     transcendence **this** world's context acknowledged

THWIILASAQBẄ indeed passage toward transparency
New learnings not teachings of the game
Touching understanding
        memory laid on eyes
                a
        film

By which **all-seeing**

(AVISTAVARZERVAIRYU)

fifth sketch, crossroads of the senses]

he begins   returns

moment   one place   exilic   he was

visitations the will pursued   his station   in spite ignorance
comes forward the interpreting angel

birth overlap to all connexions
THWIILASAQBẄ
enables passage thru Goddess
AVISTAVARZERVAIRYU
shows
in one limited gaze his first entering this world   basalt basins pools of
water caught him out of frames and diadems the vision he fell thru

purports crystalizations at the fire now

blood as water transforming fire   age compels him
see   origin his own sight   mathesis only cinematic   centers
the desert of rock   base chemical source persisted within passage because
of   THWIILASAQBẄ

passage he sees is *Iblis*   falling the thrown sense of his
coming into world not entirely demonic   except his *own* demon
        from
this entire prophetic tradition   shaman's root   directed
toward wrong   age now passed

        being alone his actualization of thought's prophetic
        for which thought and not frames
        not calculation but relation
        extension origin
        his agency
        THWIILASAQBẄ

sixth sense *CINEMAGE* (emergence)]

          parousia   Παρουσία   presence of dance around fire
then subsequent leap into fire
         passage

            unfolds now *miraj*
               reaching up into   connexion

THWIILASAQBẄ & MURMUR

Multitudes   birds
Capable dialogue and counsel
Squalor of ruins smoke flame
Parsing flow ascension
                original birth
Cycling
        wheeling wings
            wheels within wheels
        pattern
                    interpreting heat smoke squalor
                            murmur of migration
        ribboned trail weaving false eternities demonic lying tongues

Connects shoulders
            sounding echoic dimensions of RORZHNAN

        AVISTAVARZERVAIRYU's relative infinity in open
                blaring light without horizon
            pages interpreting invisible book
                design
                        migratory   ancient
                evolutionary
                        paired to the pairing birds co-notationally

seventh   ]

upward the entire sense divine and what centers
SEVLESMEHT

however
the question of individual cannot either be
downwardly impressive   or upwardly expressing   two positions in
common magic pneumatic gesture ZAS for so long embodied the world fell
into belief of disbelief itself by his two-ness

not an
unbodily proposition the individual puts forth   gesture one with
breath plays suspension of air and aether which was at the formation first
Earth first human   mutually dependent   *Qi* or middle   meso-
celestial empire earth air is and always was

individual
out of which the entire system of systems inventions
have birth in fire as fuel of light   and emptiness   a brief breath
entire worlds en-cycled

inventions
of humans as well mineral biological worlds also "conceived" in wheel
evolving descent really ascent into air   either principle or   belief
carried sub specie or   curren-
cy of image body might hold when visited by light   enlightened
so toward itself   site for breath's spell   re-suscitation its
origin

scratch]

                    previous aeon's identifications psychology of a magician's
casted spell   cast to be once again   spit from pneuma as parousia

reflected theophanic assembly SEVLESMEHT now holds   not first not
last but because he's cast
                           out
            out of it the only way to understand the gone senses of the
present age   time which cannot be retrieved by the past of the past
but in the coming past   visage of vision able to render image to this
movement of ascension   burning and   descension
                    fuels earthly angelic movement by thoroughly
covering each reveal

RE-MANTICISING IMAGE

ZAS the sublimation of all intents and purposes the demon of history lyed into
our skins deepening deathless endless speech seeking enfold you me more into
the phenomenal world as his phenomenon

        MOIRA   sublime carrier of that egoic cogitating
So then
       PLNIPLOI   entered to level life toward himself
                  prophetic by the phenomenon of self alone

Yet out of like lonely isolation
Desolate casting spell and lungful potion
Recipe   un-acknowledging beauty
Played the role of roles until

                 f i r e

     refractions of the star RORZHNAN
           incestual recognitions process
       distance into nearness
         numinal disinterestedness
           ensnaring any other mantic antic by this one

So fire

       ejaculating SEVLESMEHT

Threw his essence to burning conveyors

Fueling witness to light's creation

Whereby dark and night

         self-impregnation might

Turn three worlds humanity's thought

        toward inevitability

Closer to any pantheon

        by luminescent spunk

Out of this waiting prophetic image of engine

Mankind's inventory of invention

Rolling flames from wheels gears foretelling dynamism

     shot

        into hinge beauty distilled

THWIILASAQBẄ

s-ketching these entries]

come darken signature (s)

tenth sketch]

toward doctorate SEVLESMEHT realizes he belongs to
tradition foundation hard empiricism vanished empire appearance of witch-
doctor and shaman   both apparitions docetic attributes of transparent
attitudes light out of dark dark out of light   last note in one become
first note tone in the other   prophetic movement various transpositions
resemble groupings modes Messiaen and his play with composition alongside
open ear-canal toward birdsong captured the *quartet* itself over and over
many limited "impossible" modes yet together or in composition
portray openings toward totality whereby flights but actually symphonia of sight
found the birthplace of sight   each original sighting correspondence with
various cosmogonic light-sources order of angels issuing THWIILASAQBW̊
yet assembly made according to correspondence the
person of AVISTAVARZERVAIRYU Goddess of absolute time   she out of
circles spheres nor placed in them by mere operations or functions   other
than prophetic passage order person attending the pantheon surpasses its
number by ingenious passage   "charm of the impossible" not extended
fallacy of empiricism (that speech) nor simply a turn of phrase by which
we know someone   is embodiment swallowing all four directions this
trimester thinks as it encounters thought by experience we neither forbid nor
give to speaking voices without that tongue

eleventh sketch]

creation of self-tardiness delay in the progress of the world unconscious revolu-
tion begun to pitch the angelic against human history   albeit denied by any
and all epochs ages the very same cast-away non-purpose contains seed to all
future reasonings in the cloaca of the brain-case
                    somewhat hard to understand while empire in full swing here
now simplicity smoke air fire light wheeling iconostatic existence SEVLESMEHT
who has no need for onto-theology education's purpose nor logos but the
docetic enterprise of transparency   seeing thru all   portioning
event every substance into one passage THWIILASAQBẄ to attain the presence
of AVISTAVARZERVAIRYU
                        once thought contention even polemic dissolves
in her mode   birds a permanence of associative song modes of trans-
posed scales keys and harmonies   all within multitude or mass as at one
time blockage the sun or light at another time opening toward light measuring
echoing light's apparitions within person who tends the smoke-hole as well the
fire below   stoking creation thru embodiment of image and image's home
in flux thru THWIILASAQBẄ   comes
                        future in form of mode of the impossible

31

twelfth sketch]   this cinema made to show every age in one?
                       this visualization hanging over us
                                              prepared disappearance?

at what point along egoic implant from the badly ended past has SEVLESMEHT
learned his see-thru?   he is part of the fire now tongue a bird-congregated
assembly   adoptive of THERSEYN's backward movement   inventing
backing away casting away what is   into near habit of re-appearance
seems   yet also   seeming is   two birds not metaphor
SEVLESMEHT's head's surround of swarming masses   waves of updraft
         evolution without symbolic resonance but in his own passage
time spent eating light   waiting the leap out of centerpiece   detail
trance   leading   inversion certainly the moment nothing but that
constant mirror to work into unconscious order attain SEVLESMEHT's planet
our empty ruined planet
                          black blot's appearance contains eternity?

thirteenth sketch: indivisibleness]

conscious the empty landscape
fullness of desert not conscious   we begin   began   down
in ashes hearth beneath transformed body SEVLESMEHT given his seed to
updraft   flue   opening into place light a feeling
pinioned sockets arms keep bodies aloft in the visible ebb and
tide   how murmuration extends tongue out to fingers limited bond made
illimitable by many bird-bodies incessantly calling up the same beginning
combined limitations joining chorus body focus melodic harmonics feelings
envious orgy all souls within empirical captivity
SEVLESMEHT puts memories into hole smoke light shapes unconscious
vectors for Adamic renewal

singular soul SEVLESMEHT   collection of transient
birds opening opacities at the end of empire

empiricism ghost swallowed itself so many times became
metaphysical assumption SEVLESMEHT shaped in his own inutility
prophesizes the coming bodies of light as Anthropos in Pleistocene expanse

degradations toward exile further into exile he could hear the voice of
AVISTAVARZERVAIRYU
passed as passage now passage in
docetism of uncertainty primevality Earth glimpsed in THWIILASAQBẄ

                primitive expanse desire updraft flue leads to
amassed birds in murmuration   primal desire Adam's   announces
demand presentation the Angel of the deadest passing God
             desire leap horizon so vast passage   spheres as wings   god
inexistent for human flight non-existent   presentation eyes
releases him from docetic cycles   into finality   physical horizon
Angel's face no longer considered prophetic rather his person

        flies updraft lands on his own two feet
                                sense whole before
reconstituted form of forms correspondence to Angelic light manifestation
transposable SEVLESMEHT now is

        primeval triad   **νοῦς**   **ψυχή**   and **πνεῦμα**   re-engaged
THWIILASAQBẄ   prime-eval composition the first forever time
Angelic transposable figure   negation shadow human animal
        SEVLESMEHT now synonymous emergence
THWIILASAQBẄ transposition of Sophia brilliant light passage
                AVISTAVARZERVAIRYU

Now finally *EPIPHANATIC* joining: Quartet for the End of time

"Their melodic contours, those of merles especially, surpass
human imagination in fantasy …. volleys and trills of our
little prophets of immaterial joy …"
Messiaen, *La technique de mon langage musical (1944)*

Four birds   cross roads

Blackbird Nightingale Merle and Chat

Out the Abyss Time emerges

Prefigures

Depth the muscular movement

Opacity Anthropoidal
       THWIILASAQBẄ
             epiphany   banality
                   opens its Angelic inventory
       crosses   crossing light
       updraft   changeover   end of the prophet/shaman

shaman wears each invention of light

                         ultimately diaphanaticly
      merges nor suspends mirroring by will
      nor empire
                its cousin historical (outdated) reason the prophetic hand
thought to master by way of a static presence in the present tensings of time's
habits

     our world   given to ordering symbolic articulation
           full
Deserted
      music the heart's dark cloister

Assumes end of time all the time

Symbolic Restitution

Such difficult understanding in the unreachable

o that gods attached

stories narrations voices

told tell still

disappearance of light

acknowledging self for whom

rhythm

expands contracts

recognizable parts

as they are also solely whole

CASTS <----> TARGETS

Human soul in follow-thru
                SEVLESMEHT
Crossing fire

Pneumatic haunts ZAS
                SHIRU's mouth
Exhalant exegesis

Esoteric sense
                sound
Transposes landscape's exoterica

Each scape
                in need
You find

What star
                centers
Multiplies
                understands
Reveals

Images funding
                    housed dug
Beneath symbolic register

"I named
                    horizon fiery body
Dim historical light-source"

Invention the profiter
          SEVLESMEHT
                    re-creates

Rock of ages

          no longer ...

                    ...birds...

NOTHINGNESS

Overcome
                    empire's ending?
Names evocation's subtracting

                                            soul?

Nothingness
                    attachment material splendor
          horizon views   deep tank sounds absented time
                    we the assemblage various nuclei
          swimming void pre-existences
                    unknown to once notable poets?

The capture of prophet by empire
                    SEVLSEMEHT the proving ground
                    beyond profits the loss
Providence an uncertain Angel
                    buried burning skin
                              light the crossing
                              holds darkly

Five attributes sustaining fire evokes
    eternal existent humanity
        SEVLESMEHT correspondent voice
Themselves birds the bird's
        eternity shaped

                once?

Our time and place a play upon after-meaning

Personified exteriority exilic
    relative destiny
Lost assigned species
        recurring moment's
Seed-stem returns form to
    labyrinthine flue

        detonated bloom-burst

the last sketch]

       between old magician ZAS whose *pneumatic* arc up to *nous* sought
to gain power thru violent propaganda   down that *nous* it was old
AHNÁHR traveled the invisible realm prophetic invention which shaped
the machine-age the historical arc then down to firing missiles   valo-
rized by MOIRA   advent brought about medial range a beginning
short-lived nothingness totaled ruined evacuated the entire human empire
from Earth   made way for mesocosmics SEVLESMEHT realized in his
pawning role after fullness the desert's horizon   *psyche* by which songs
SHIRU would finally interpret and sing

                        THWIILASAQBẄ
bridging fullness the final Sophia   she in whom no attitude *projected*
toward *idea* man
          AVISTAVARZERVAIRYU   embodies   garment of light
                        interpenetrating origin perdurably

Songs SHIRU sang to bring AHNÁHR into fullness

Distant invisibility
          final circulation
      not breath
    love undying
                intimacy threads
      mutual music hears

THERSEYN
        hidden figure
Emerges unwanton currency

Able

from afar

AHNÁHR

Needed   neither now desires

        "themselves"

nor thread's appearance's

        sign

                midst transit's aim

        coming back again

*"Delay no more" *temps* replaces *World*:

Notes on the blackbird's advice for the Quartet's score

What end mystery   un-seeking discernment of event?

       MAN

             dumb as a door-knob

      "The special rhythms, independent of the meter, powerfully contribute to the effect of banishing the temporal."   M. *Composer's Preface*

             Apotheosis of one offspring into note lineage the Father
encircles the camp with barbed wire   heaven stalag-titic construction at the
start   near war's beginning   world begun thanatos undifferentiated
milky utterance without touch
         sin the capital by which its other manifests only in "revelation"
            uncloaked kept the capsule of a joke
       secrecy internment too slips into language the birds
rising offal or burned off essence no longer any "use"

                    EARTH   evolution of all wars
                              the very name of peace
                                        posits spunk creation perver-
sion which spreads out all spreading   upward   outward
"speaks to us"   instead of

                              . . . .

"non-retrogradable rhythms"

                         interesting most important to note Black Kali the
appearance of just such a moment in adversity   the very springs of
created life itself

          **so Xristos counterpart would be a falsity thus monstrous
destroyer of life by his releasing war within a Logos as central generation of
deathless MAN**

The note which descendants of saurian form sound contains **end** of MAN

      we can hear   however   crossing tongue large
throat out of which Kali spreads her tongue to lick up all false statement
proposition contains an ever-widening uncontrollable multiplication of Lilith's
substitution by way of EDN

the flip of the spread   Kali rose to as Priestess
of power chakras and circles   re-involved MAN in celestial pre-
substitutional apotheotic idiocy   obsessive thought hearing and not-
hearing as it thinks its unending the same as smoke's discharge

                    "Whether read from right to left or from left to
                    right, the order of their values remains the same. This
                    feature exists in all rhythms that can be divided into
                    two groups of retrograde related to each other by a
                    "common" value."   M. *Composer's Preface*

Jesus the most common desire ever created: the wish to **be** God
                    takes polyphony by common stress (when stressed as
total value translation of the term of delay in revelation alone   not
interactivations of circuitry pro-creative participation)   spoils it in
production of a look the entire embodiment of empire thus
                    uniform
                              Black Kali comes to meet now over
and over to rescue PLNIPLOI in the mirror they both have never really seen but
certainly heard the rumor of each in the other   possibly in egg-shape
of that non-retrogradable rhythm or span endangering even themselves

                         . . . .

ABYSS OF THE BIRDS

solo

flailing instrument to find the gate

Only SEVLESMEHT when he leapt into black fire   (hūp-ah!)

exhausted thru and thru by vaulted nothingness

his wish connected updraft toward one star

perfect timing joined new crystallization

seeing more than one before after black meaning's hold en-

cyphers

in its blackness

flue her tongue reaches thru his "head"

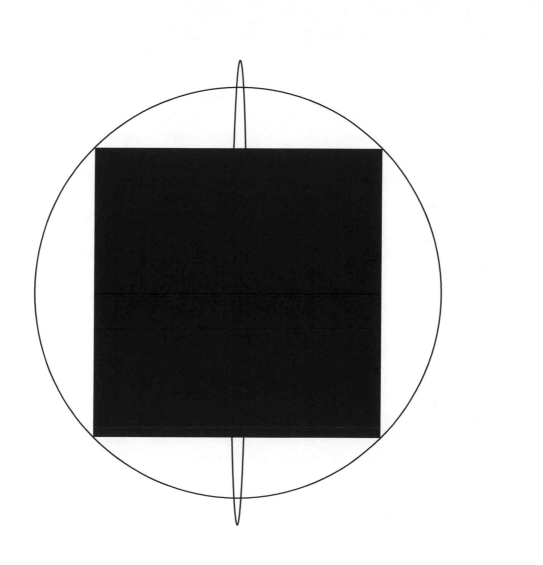

After-Meaning:
Messaien's Transposable Mode

In the sense of one composer's famous incarceration—made so from the composition he put into motion—internment translates our own time, whether it be at a loss to recover historical definition or even personal memorization; whether it is deemed to be competent or even a performance of this or that art, captivation still can be acknowledged. Acknowledged in the hope it might rise to the register of a recognition, the music played out from one group of musicians to assembled and condensed audiences.

Quartet for the End of Time was begun before Messaien's imprisonment by an invading German army that eventually occupied France (1940).

It is the recognition of two things at once, a palindromic (retrogradable & non-retrogradable) rhythm, and the Limited Transposition of pitch or scale which intersects with birdsong Messaien understood as the time signature to the composition. In other words, the absence of denotative time for a given bar of music was left out of the score. Instead, rhythms as well as pitch at the center of each movement allude to "impossibilities," limited scales and activities (forward as well as backward) of the composition in order to furnish a vocabulary that continually criss-crosses.

A limited or set group of musical components, repeating their own signatures as instances of their complete limit (much the same as a note is a complete and "finite" unit) makes the actual score funnel into the "abyss" of each of their occasions.

Messaien had already begun the score for what would become the central movement of the Quartet, "Abyss of the Birds," before his capture and subsequent imprisonment at Stalag 8A in Poland. So the idea of both a "serial" approach to building the language of a score and the phenomenal interface with birds and birdsong had already entered the composer's field of interest.

Could it be the blackbird, the *merle,* he had already identified with the space of a timelessness, is eternity itself?

It would be in keeping with Messaien's devout Catholicism that such a "transposition" would scale his own involvement with Xrist, as well as the world, just as it is found by each of us (on our own terms).

The intention inherent in the cross, then, is not simply a centerpiece to the "faith" of any one religion, as if it owned even the limited modes of its own understandings; rather, in those limited terms and vocabularies, those utterances, the eternal shows the listener the true meaning of doctrinal practice come to an "end".

In this use of an "end" (of time) everywhere, the various terms, incomprehensible by themselves, become completely understandable when inverted, turned around, made "retrogradable". (SEVLESMEHT).

E n d

BOOK 6

Anatomical Sketches

T THILLEMAN is the author of *Three Sea Monsters (Our History of Whose Image)* in which journal entries and poetic sequences investigate the legacy of Pound's redactions to Fenollosa's original manuscript version of *The Chinese Written Character as a Medium for Poetry*; *Onönyxa & Therseyn* (opening for an extended work, *Anatomical Sketches,* of which *Sevlesmeht & the Birds* is the sixth book); *Snailhorn (fragments),* a 360 poem cycle utilizing vedic transitions in celestial to allegorical articulation; and the novel *Gowanus Canal, Hans Knudsen.* His literary essay/memoir, *Blasted Tower,* was issued by Shakespeare & Co./ Toad Suck in 2013. tt's pastel drawings and readings are archived at conchwoman.wordpress.com.

Made in the USA
Charleston, SC
04 February 2015